Make Money Fiverr

Complete Step-by-Step Guide to Make a Full Time Income!

Introduction 1

Chapter 1: What is Fiverr? Some Basics to Understand 2

Chapter 2: Why Fiverr Is a Great Platform for You 5

Chapter 3: Getting Started with Fiverr 9

Chapter 4: Advertising and Finding Customers 12

Chapter 5: Pricing, Schemes and Customer Reviews 17

Chapter 6: Using Fiverr for Music/ Freelance Writing/ Designing 21

Chapter 7: Mistakes to Avoid On Fiverr 28

Chapter 8: The Importance of Scaling and Automating Gigs .. 34

Chapter 9: Virtual Assistants and How They Can Help 42

Chapter 10: Advanced Fiverr Marketing Tips for Success 49

Chapter 11: How to Be Successful in a Gig Realm 58

Conclusion 62

Special Invitation! 63

FREE Bonus Videos! 64

© Copyright 2016 - All rights reserved.

In no way is it legal to reproduce, duplicate, or transmit any part of this document in either electronic means or in printed format. Recording of this publication is strictly prohibited and any storage of this document is not allowed unless with written permission from the publisher. All rights reserved.

The information provided herein is stated to be truthful and consistent, in that any liability, in terms of inattention or otherwise, by any usage or abuse of any policies, processes, or directions contained within is the solitary and utter responsibility of the recipient reader. Under no circumstances will any legal responsibility or blame be held against the publisher for any reparation, damages, or monetary loss due to the information herein, either directly or indirectly.

Respective authors own all copyrights not held by the publisher.

Legal Notice:
This book is copyright protected. This is only for personal use. You cannot amend, distribute, sell, use, quote or paraphrase any part or the content within this book without the consent of the author or copyright owner. Legal action will be pursued if this is breached.

Disclaimer Notice:
Please note the information contained within this document is for educational and entertainment purposes only. Every attempt has been made to provide accurate, up to date and reliable complete information. No warranties of any kind are expressed or implied. Readers acknowledge that the author is not engaging in the rendering of legal, financial, medical or professional advice.

By reading this document, the reader agrees that under no circumstances are we responsible for any losses, direct or indirect, which are incurred as a result of the use of information contained within this document, including, but not limited to, —errors, omissions, or inaccuracies.

Introduction

The Internet is now a powerful platform and goes beyond helping us seek information and connect with friends and loved ones. We can now earn a living through the Internet, provided we go about it the right way.

There are many ways in which you can make money online, such as through affiliate marketing, setting up online shops, blogging etc. But none of them are as efficient as having a Gig on Fiverr.

Fiverr is a website that allows people to pursue their passion and find work based on their skills.

It is a place where many business seekers and business employers converge to give and take work. And if you are looking to get started with Fiverr, then you have come to the right place!

We will look at the basics of Fiverr and how you can get started with it as soon as possible. We will also look at how you can turn your Fiverr business into a success story.

This book will act as your Fiverr guide and usher you into the right direction.

Let us begin.

Chapter 1: What is Fiverr? Some Basics to Understand

First and foremost, I thank you for choosing this book. In this first chapter, we will look at the purpose of Fiverr and some basic concepts that you should know about.

What is Fiverr?

Fiverr is a website that advertises itself as the world's largest marketplace for services. The Fiverr website is a place where you advertise your services and find clients who will employ you.

Started in 2010, Fiverr started off as a small website that hosted only a few buyers and sellers. However, it grew in popularity within a short period of time and within the next 2 years, Fiverr hosted 1.3 million users. It is said to have grown over 600% in business within 3 years of starting up.

Fiver is an online market place where both buyers and sellers converge to give and take services. It is a freelance marketplace where anybody can advertise and anybody can avail services. These can be small services or even micro services.

Fiverr is better referred to as an online outsourcing portal that helps clients find potential employees and vice versa.

How does it work?

Fiverr works in a pretty straightforward fashion. There are two options that are available with one being for the customers and the other one being for the clients. Each service on Fiverr is known as a gig. The customers have the chance to showcase their skills and advertise their gigs and the clients can view these and employ them. Once the client contacts the service provider and the work is discussed, the latter gets a time limit within which they should prepare and submit the work. Once the work is submitted and marked as completed, they are paid their due.

Can anyone get started with it?

Fiverr is a vast marketplace and encourages all types of people to use it. You can access it from any part of the world and have any sort of skill set to start with it. Right from students to working professionals, and housewives, just about anyone can get started with Fiverr and provide their services to a sea of clients. It is quite easy to register and get started with Fiverr so anyone can get started with it right away. Similarly, clients looking for a diverse range of work can get started with Fiverr. There is no restriction on who can and cannot start with Fiverr. We will look at this aspect in detail in a while.

What can I advertise on it?

Fiverr is a platform that encourages all types of skills and talents. So right from writing to editing to singing and also designing, you can find the right job for yourself on Fiverr. There are some standard options to choose from like writing content, writing articles, creating jingles, logos etc. You can choose from a diverse range of gigs to advertise and use each one to your advantage. Apart from the regular jobs, there can also be certain special requests that some customers might have, which they can use to request special services.

How much will I earn from it?

Earning money from Fiverr is quite easy and how much you earn will depend on your work. There is no standard earning limit and you can earn as high as $5000 a month. But for that, you will have to pick a lucrative gig and have an impressive profile to find regular clients.

There are many success stories out there and you can have one of your own depending on the skill set that you own. You need not advertise just a single gig and can have as many as you like.

How long does it take to complete a gig?

Generally, people try to finish a gig as soon as possible so that they can move to the next one. Some people take as little as 1 day and some might take 30 days. The client will have the chance to pick an option within which the work should be submitted. The standard option on the site includes 24 hours, 3 days, 7 days etc. The job profile will have a big say in the time that it will take for a person to complete a job. Sometimes, the client will affix the time frame for the job within which the service provider has to submit the work. For this, they will choose between the 1-30 days option and pick the number of days that they think is best for the job.

What about the competition?

It is impossible for an online marketplace to not have any competition. It is obvious that many people will advertise their gigs on the platform and you will have to face stiff competition. But given how much work actually needs to get done, you might not have to stand in line for your work to be reviewed and employed. You might have to work a little hard at the very beginning to make your mark but will get progressively easier for you to hit it off on Fiverr.

Should I quit my day job for it?

That decision is up to you to make. There are some people who take up Fiverr gigs as their day job and quit their previous jobs for it. If you think your Fiverr gigs have picked up traction and you are able to earn a substantial amount from it then you can take it up full time.

Chapter 2: Why Fiverr Is a Great Platform for You

When it comes to an online platform that offers people the opportunity to make money several doubts crop up in their minds. Some of these include doubts on whether they have picked the best platform to pursue and whether or not it will give them the desired output.

I'm sure you have the same doubts in your mind when it comes to Fiverr and so, here are some reasons that make Fiverr a great place to find your clients and set up your business.

Free sign up

One of the biggest advantages of Fiverr is the Free Sign Up that it offers. You don't have to pay anything towards signing up on it and can start advertising yourself within a matter of minutes. If you have had a bad experience in the past over fraudulent websites that charge you money to get started, then Fiverr is sure to help erase any such memories, for good!

Easy to use

It is obvious that people want something easy to work with as otherwise it will be quite difficult for them to manage their business. Fiverr will prove to be a good choice owing to its ease of use. You won't have to put in too much effort to understand how it works and it will all seem a bit too easy for you to set up your business. Through the course of this book, you will know how exactly to get started with your business and how you can use the website to your advantage.

Diversity

Fiverr is a website that provides an opportunity to many people with diverse skills. This means that you don't have to have a particular skill set alone and can get started with your skill set. So whether you are a designer or a singer, Fiverr will give you the chance to use your talent to the fullest. You can help create jingles, write content, design logos etc. There is no limit on the things that you can do with the help of Fiverr and you are sure to remain busy with it for a long, long time

Follow your passion

One of the main criteria that people look for when they wish to start a business is, whether it allows them to follow their passion. If the platform helps them exploit their hidden talent, then they are sure to take it up and exploit it. Fiverr is one such place that allows you to pursue your passion and follow your dreams. Whether it is a flair for writing or a talent for singing, you can hone your skill and start making money with it through Fiverr. You will have the chance to be happy with whatever that you do.

Pricing

The pricing policy of Fiverr is quite easy to understand and exploit. As you know, you can work on the site and advertise it for $5, at least. Depending on how much you think your service is worth, you can price it accordingly. You don't have to worry about thinking too long about pricing your services and can look up at what price your competition is offering their work at. Based on it, you can price your services accordingly.

Flexibility

The flexibility that Fiverr offers, adds another advantage to picking the site. This means that you can work for a few days, take a break and then work again. There is no rigid time line to when you need to report to work. The choice is completely yours and you can pick your own work timings. This aspect is especially useful for those looking to work part time. Flexible timings are also ideal for those wanting to work with foreign clients. Remember that people from all over the world sign up with Fiverr and you can choose to work with a local client or pick one from abroad.

Community

There are also a vast number of buyers and you will not have to go after them in search of work. They will themselves come to you and provide you with work. It is safe to say that there will be a diverse mix of customers that you will come across and diversify your customer base. You will find both long-term users and those looking to employ temporarily. You will have the chance to pick from a diverse range of employers. The support of a community can be a big deal and Fiverr is sure to keep you happy in respect to it.

Customer support

The Fiverr customer support team is quite vast and very helpful. They will be available at any time and answer questions to help you out. Should you have any doubt, you can simply ask the question and have it answered. You can also ask for their help to fix any issues you might be facing. There are many ways of reaching out to the community and some of it includes e-mailing them, or leaving behind feedback. They will look into it and help you. If you have any issues with a client, you can e-mail the concerned team and have them look into it. You can also get in touch with some of the other Fiverr users and have your questions answered.

Withdrawing money

There are some platforms that do not have a flexible money withdrawing policy. They expect you to reach a certain amount before the money can be withdrawn. But at Fiverr, there is no such rule. You will be able to withdraw the money within 14 days after the task is marked completed and for top rated sellers, the time period is 7 days. We will look at how you can withdraw money from your Fiverr account in a later chapter of this book.

These form the different advantages of working with Fiverr but are not limited to just these. Once you start using Fiverr, you will get acquainted with the other benefits.

Chapter 3: Getting Started with Fiverr

In order to get started with Fiverr, there are a few basic steps that you should follow. Let us look at them in this chapter.

Step 1: The very first step is to register yourself on the website. For that, you should visit this Page. As you can see, you can register with your email, Facebook account or your Google+ account. You can then choose a *USERNAME* for yourself. But remember that once chosen, you cannot change it. So, you should think it through. Once completed, you will get a link in your email that you have to click to activate the account.

Step 2: Next, you can secure your account by choosing a security question to help secure your account. Next, you should add your PayPal account details. It is best for you to link your PayPal account, as that is the easiest and safest place for you to get your money.

Step 3: Next, you can work on your profile. Remember to fill in all the required fields and give away honest information. You can manage your public profile and choose what you want your audience to see and what not. However, it is best to not add in any personal information like your address or phone number, as many people will be able to see what you put in. There, you will also have the option of picking the language. This language will help your customers communicate with you easily.

Step 4: The next step is for you to start creating your gigs. Gigs, as you know, stand for your sales pitch. It is what you will use to attract your customers. You can go to **Selling>Create a Gig.** There, you should first add a title to the gig in about 80 characters. Then, select the category and sub-category that befits the gig. You have to then select an image that suits the gig. Next, you can add in the description of the gig. This is probably the most important part, as your clients will finalize you based on what you add in. You will have a limit of 1200 characters. Next, you can add in the metadata that will make your gig SEO friendly. You can then add in any desired files and fill in all the other important fields. Remember to set a live portfolio as that will help showcase your work.

Step 5: The next step is to price your gig. You should choose a gig package that will help you choose both the price of the gig and the time that it will take to complete it. This is important, as your client should know when they would get their work.

Step 6: Once done, you can start working. But before that, you should spread the word about your Fiverr profile. You can paste the link on all your social media platforms in order to educate people about it. Remember that this is an important step, as people should know about your gigs. The more effort you put into exposure of the gigs as well as other marketing efforts, the more likely people are to purchase it.

Step 7: Once your order is placed by a client, you should begin work on it. You should look at the time period that they have given you and work accordingly. Once your work is done, you have to deliver it. For that, go to your dashboard and find **TO-DO**. There, you should click on **Deliver Now** and have the work delivered.

Step 8: You can manage your sales. You can go to it through **Selling>Managing Sales.** The first option you see there will be priority option that refers to the work that is cancelled or late orders. Next, you will see the new option that refers to the new orders that you have received. The Active orders refer to the orders that you are now working upon. Late orders refer to the ones that you had to submit 24 hours before and are still waiting. Delivered refers to the orders that you have submitted to the buyer but have not been marked complete as yet. Completed stands for the orders that you have completed and submitted. Cancelled are for the orders that you cancelled.

Step 9: Once your work is delivered, the client will mark it as complete and you will be paid for it. Once you are paid, you can withdraw the money after 14 days.

Step 10: Fiverr faces is a new feature that you can exploit. It refers to an app that helps create a caricature of your face. This is an interesting feature and will help you create a caricature that you can use as your profile. You will be charged for it and the sum will depend on the delivery time that you choose for it.

These form the different simple steps that you can follow in order to get started with your Fiverr account and start your business.

Chapter 4: Advertising and Finding Customers

It is important to advertise yourself and get word of your gig out there. There are success stories of people earning $5000 and above in a single month and that is only possible if you spread the word of your gigs out there and notify people about your work.

Here are a few things that you can do to guarantee a large audience.

SEO

The first and foremost thing you need to understand is SEO and its usefulness. As you know, SEO stands for search engine optimization and is meant to help your gig turn up as the first result on a search engine. It is extremely important for you to make use of keywords that are most likely going to get typed in by your clients. The more the keyword matches, the higher your gig will be placed. You should also fill in the metadata and make use of appropriate headings that contain the important keywords. If you are not sure about any of it, you can ask an expert about it or take the help of an SEO expert to help you out. You can also look up some of the things others are doing and employ the same tricks. Funny enough, you can also find SEO experts directly on Fiverr itself!

Blog

Having a blog always helps with promoting your online presence. For this, you should start a blog and write on interesting topics pertaining to the kind of work you enjoy and your passions. You can start a free blog on blogger and start writing. If you already have a blog, then you can mention your Fiverr gig and divert your audience. If you don't have a big enough audience, then you can look and connect with popular bloggers and get them to write for you or be a guest blogger for you. That way, you will have the chance to get all of his or her fans to check out your Fiverr gig and at least half of them might consider you.

Facebook

Facebook is the world's biggest social networking site and has billions of users. You can promote your Fiverr gig on Facebook and inform all your friends about it. You also have the option of creating a separate and dedicated page for your gig. You can create a Facebook Page where you can write everything about your gig, the services you offer and share appropriate links. You can send an invite to all your friends to like it and also ask them to share it with theirs and them with theirs etc. That way, you can obtain a lot of likes for your gig and build a large audience.

Twitter

Twitter is the next best social networking site that you can pick to advertise your gigs. As you know, twitter has millions of users and a worldwide reach. You can create a separate twitter page for your company and share links of your gigs. As you know, you can tweet about it and get others to retweet. That is sure to get you get noticed by many people, who might be based all over the world. But don't limit it to just writing about your gig. You have to give people a reason to visit your page and writing about trending topics is sure to help you.

Google+

Google+ is now gaining popularity owing to its ease of use and the sharing options that it provides. It is as simple as clicking on the icon that appears on the left hand side of Gmail and people will be redirected to your Google+ page. They can then check it out and go to your Fiverr page. Remember to have an impressive landing page that will raise people's curiosity. You should share other interesting links as well as that is sure to make your users stay on the page.

LinkedIn

Linked is another place where you can promote your gigs. LinkedIn, as you know, is a site for professionals. You too can create a professional page for your company and add in links to your gigs. You have to connect with other professionals and also other companies. Don't wait for them to look for you and connect and send them connections by yourself. You can also try the professional set up option where you will have to pay a little fee but your gig will reach all the right places.

YouTube

It is an absolute must for you to have your own YouTube channel if you wish to advertise your business efficiently. You can add videos of your gigs that provide information about it, describe its aspects etc. You can also add links of your gigs in the description so that people can visit your page. You must also actively participate in the comments section and answer questions. And don't forget the call to action message that you have to provide at the end of every video. People should be reminded to check out your link that you add at the bottom.

Instagram

Instagram is where you can share pictures with the world. You can take quality pictures of the work that you provide and share the pictures on it. You can then share the links to these pictures on other sites such as Facebook and twitter. It is great to get some of your clients to help out as well and ask them to take pictures of the work that you provided to them.

Forums

It is important to participate in forum discussions. There are many forums where you can share links to your gigs. You can answer any questions that are getting asked on these forums and then add in a link to your gig. You should try and incorporate the gig in your answer so that the message is delivered subtly. You should try and visit as many forums as possible and not think of any of them as not being worthy. You never know where you might get your next client or group of clients.

Press release

Press releases refer to releasing information about your gigs in the press. This is possible if you know anybody who works at the press and will help you out. If you don't, you can contact the editor to help you have it released. It is best to choose the online platform of the tabloid. You must create an interesting headline and then mention the details of your gig. You can then have it printed or published. This is sure to get you noticed by a lot of people. You can also share the link of the release on all your social media sites. All of these social media outlets mentioned increases the exposure of your gigs and can all be outsourced by finding social media marketers directly on Fiverr!

Average score

It is important for your average rating to be high in order for you to show up on top when someone searches for you. Many buyers have cited looking at the average ratings score to find the best one. It is best to have the score between 4.5 and 5 so that people are impressed by it. You have to keep yourself in all your clients' good books and get them to give you a good rating each time. Even if you do get a 3 or 3.5, they should be much fewer compared to the 4s and 5s that you have.

There are several things you can do to increase your rating. Giving additional value to the customer by providing extra services free of charge or bonuses for being a repeated customer will be rewarded with higher ratings. Some bonuses can be easily added once you build a streamlined system. For example, if you were creating e-book covers as your gig, you can set up a template file to automatically convert your designed 2-d cover into 3-d to add as a bonus. Once the template is created, it takes almost no time to create the 3-d cover, which will definitely impress the customers!

Samples

When you send the samples to your clients, you should send them your best work. You should also send links to your website and other important files and links. It is best to get referrals from your current customers, as they will know others interested in the same. You can also get them to praise you, as many people are influenced by others opinions.

As mentioned earlier about setting up templates to provided additional free of charge bonuses, one way to drastically increase the referral rate is by joining different facebook groups that go hand in hand with the kind of Fiverr gig you are offering, and offering a free gig to a few members. This is a fast an effective way to boost your rank and ratings. For example, if your gig was creating e-book covers, you can join different self publishing groups and offer a free cover to a few members. You can also let them know that if they refer you to someone else, they will get a discount on their next order, as well as the person who got referred. This builds a strong foundation of loyal and happy customers early on!

These form the different ways in which you can advertise your work and spread word to as many different people as possible.

Chapter 5: Pricing, Schemes and Customer Reviews

In the previous chapter, we looked at how you can make use of social media to spread word about your gigs. In this one, we will look at pricing strategies and also how you can deal with bad customer reviews.

Pricing it right

Pricing gigs is one of the most important aspects of Fiverr. It is important for you to choose the right price for the services. As you know, you can choose either $5 or more for your services. The $5 tag is for all those services that are quite easy to perform and might take less than an hour to finish. Say for example writing 200 words for someone. But if you provide time-consuming services such as creating instructional videos, then you must charge accordingly. Generally, the best way to decide on the price is by looking at what others are charging. You can assess whether you are over or under pricing for your services. As you know, you can choose from the different packages that are provided on the site. You have to slowly increase your rates depending on the reviews and the work quality that you provide.

Special offers

You should indulge in some lucrative strategies in order to get more and more customers to buy from you. As you know, everybody loves discounts and freebies. You too should make use of these schemes to attract your clients and keep them happy. Some of these schemes include giving away a special discount like 10% off if the client orders your service in bulk. You can also give away free service if they cross a certain limit like 15 or 20. Another good idea is to give away some personalized merchandise as a gift for being a regular customer. You can also tie up with another Fiverr and come up with buy my service and get a discount on theirs type of schemes. You can be as creative as you like with your special offers and attract a diverse group of clients.

Why ratings/ reviews matter

When it comes to the ratings and reviews that clients leave behind, you have to try and have as many good ones as possible. Your future clients will take these reviews and ratings very seriously and choose you only if they think you are worth their money. As you know, you cannot expect to always come across great clients that will leave behind great reviews. It is tough to have a consistent winning streak and you should be ready for a few bad clients/ reviews as well. A good seller will know what to expect well in advance and can continue work accordingly. When another client is looking for you, your ratings and reviews will show up as the first thing under your picture. So, it is important to make a good impression and if not first, then at least remain in the top 5 results.

Changing review

As was mentioned earlier, it is not possible for you to always get good reviews all the time. You will also get some bad reviews that can bring down your worth. This can be a bad thing and might crush your confidence. So, it is important to try and eliminate a bad review. One way of doing it is by speaking with the client and asking him or her to edit the review. Sometimes, speaking with them and telling them how it will impact your business might make them change their mind. You can send them a message about the review and ask them to change the review or rating for you. But remember to get it done as soon as possible as you might not have too much time to get it removed or changed. You will see the option in your orders page at the very bottom. Reviews are a very important thing not only on Fiverr, but any kind of website that offers services. They are a good indication of what to expect when ordering these services and it greatly benefits the consumers. However, the service providers like yourself can greatly benefit from the reviews as well. These reviews will accurately tell you what is working and what is not working. Take the time to read the negative reviews and review the quality of work you are providing. Was the review accurate? Did you do something wrong? Take the input and learn from it. Many of the top gigs on Fiverr offer top notch customer service and will correct their work until the customer is completely satisfied. Add value to the customers, and you will be rewarded and will be on your way to getting a top rated seller badge!

Cancelling an order

Many times, you and a buyer might hit it off well and everything might go according to plan. However, a problem might arise later and you might want to discontinue the project. In such a case, you and your buyer can opt for a mutual cancel. That way, you won't have to cancel the order yourself. However, if your client is being difficult and not agreeing to mutually cancel then you have the option to cancel it yourself. This is a unique feature of Fiverr where the seller is given the option to cancel and is better known as force cancelling. This will, however, impact your rating but you can successfully stop the client from giving you a bad review. After all, you have to do everything in your power to keep your account as clean as possible and away from negative reviews. Sometimes it is worth cancelling the order opposed to having an extremely negative review displayed for your gig.

Rivals

There are many cases of rivals trying to ruin your game. There might be some people who will claim to be clients but will actually be your rivals. They might purchase your service and give you a bad rating on purpose. In fact, they might not take the submission at all and leave behind a bad rating. It is important for you to find out if that really is the case. You must look at the client's profile and see what he or she is up to. If you find out that they provide the same service as you, then you should take action against them.

Customer support

The best way to bring them to justice is by telling customer support about it. You should show them the review and rating that the rival has left behind. You should also tell them that the person is purposely trying to sabotage you. They will look into the matter and help resolve it. It might take a week or so but it will be well worth the effort.

These form the different pricing and customer review aspects of Fiverr.

Chapter 6: Using Fiverr for Music/ Freelance Writing/ Designing

By now, you must have understood the basics of Fiverr, getting started with it and also how you can promote yourself. Now, let us look at top gigs that will help you earn a good sum of money on a monthly basis.

Writing

Freelance writing is quite popular on Fiverr. Here are some gigs that you can try out.

Article writing

Article writing refers to writing 100 to 500 worded articles for your client. They will give you the topic and might also give you a few keywords that you should incorporate into the article. You can mention the topics that you are good at, so that the client will find it easy to hire you. Most of these services are charged between $5 and $10.

Content writing

Content writing is the next option that you can choose. Content writing is slightly different from article writing and you will have to have diverse knowledge on a specific subject. That will help you fill in content and write informative stuff. These are generally commissioned by people trying to fill their websites. You can mention your topic of expertise. Content writing is priced according to the quality of the service and also based on the turnover time. Depending on the time that you take to complete orders, you can take up as many of these projects as possible.

EBooks

EBooks are the next type of writing projects that you can advertise on Fiverr. EBooks are electronic books that people can download from the web and read. If you are good at a particular topic, then you can mention it and make it easier for your clients to find you. EBooks can vary in length and the topics can differ in terms of difficulty level. You can charge them accordingly.

Editing/ proofreading

Apart from writing the content, you can also edit or proofread it. Editing refers to correcting any formatting mistakes in the book and proofreading calls for reading it to find any grammatical or spelling errors. If you are good at both, then you can offer both of these services. Some clients might ask you to add in pictures to the content or provide a cover page etc. You can charge for all these services individually. Proofreading is quite popular on Fiverr and you can charge from $5 onwards.

Videos

The next popular category involves making use of videos. This is probably easier than the previous option and all you have to do is tap into your creative side. Here are some services that you can offer to clients.

Video introductions

Video introductions are quite popular these days. These refer to introductions that you create for your client or any other video that they will ask you to make. Some might ask for specific videos and give you specific instructions. Some might give you the freedom to create something based on your understanding of the client. Videos are generally charged between $5 and $50 depending on the amount of work and animation that goes into making them. You can charge higher if you think your creations are really creative and unique.

Video greetings

Video greetings are all the rage these days. Right from wishing on Christmas to birthdays and New Year, people prefer to send across video greetings. It is all the more important to customize these and include specific messages in each. You can create these video greetings for your clients. You can use a few standard templates and ask your client to choose one. Right now, most top sellers are selling these for $5.

Video ads

Video ads are also an option. You can create ads for products by studying them. It will especially be easy for you if you already use the products. Your client might also ask you to add in a product description video or a demonstration video. These ads are also charged between $5 and $50 depending on the amount of work that goes into it.

Hold your sign

Hold your sign is now gaining popularity. You can offer to hold a sign with a personal message written on it. The client will provide you with the message and you can write it on a piece of cardboard or some other piece of paper and hold it. Most people choose funny videos where you dance around or do something silly with the board. These range between $5 and $25.

Editing/ photoshopping

You can also offer to edit videos or photoshop them. The clients will submit the videos to you and you can edit them as per the instructions. If you are good at fixing videos or adding in details, then you can offer the services for more than $5.

Music/ sound

You can also make use of music and sound to start your Fiverr business. This is great for both budding musicians and those that wish to pursue their passion for music. Here are some options for you to choose from.

Jingles and drops

Jingles are a big thing these days and many people get them done. Jingles are small compositions that people might need for their websites, apps etc. The client will specify the words that should be used in the jingle. You should have a few templates and samples ready to show to the client. These are usually charged between $5 and $25 and will depend on the length and the quality of the composition. Some people prefer to tape the jingles in studios to make it sound professional. Some also set up the camera in front of them while composing the jingle.

Songs

You need not always create short jingles and can also record entire songs if you are good at singing. It is also a choice to simply compose the music for someone. They will have full rights over it and can add a song to it. You should mention the instruments that you are good with to make it easier for them to pick you. These are charged at $5 and over.

Voice-overs

Voice-overs are the next option that you have. Voice-overs refer to saying something in a unique voice or in a specified voice. The voice can belong to a celebrity or someone famous. The client will ask you to say something in the unique voice. Some of the trending voices these days are that of the queen of England and also some singers. You can easily record the words in the specified voice and might only take you a couple of hours. These are now charged at $5.

Designing

If you are good at designing or drawing, then there is ample scope for your skills on Fiverr. Here are some things that you can do with your skill.

Logos

Creating unique and interesting logos is all the rage these days. Right from start-ups to old companies, everybody is looking for a unique logo that will help people identify their brand. If you are good with designing logos, then you can start providing the service on Fiverr. You can ask your clients to choose from specific templates or color schemes and create the logos. These logos need not always only be 2D and can also be 3D. These are generally charged $5 per logo depending on the design and time taken to create.

Cartoons

It is a great idea to create cartoons for clients if you are good at drawing. The client will give you the subject and all you have to do is create a cartoon. Some might ask you to simply fill in color or some such special request. You can create both 2D and 3d cartoons depending on your skill and software that you possess. The former is generally charged lesser as compared to the latter. Most of these start at $5 and can go up to $100 depending on the quality of the animation and the length of the cartoons.

Caricatures

Caricatures are extremely popular these days. People like turning themselves into cartoons and sharing it with their friends and family. If you are good at free hand sketching or have created software that helps turn people's faces into caricatures, then you can advertise it on Fiverr. It is now being charged between $5 and $15 for a single caricature and $20 for two or more people. You need not always do caricatures alone and can also choose regular paintings or portraits.

Merchandise

You can offer to create custom merchandise designs for your clients. As you know, most companies like to have their label on mugs; caps, T-shirts etc. and they will look for artists to do it for them. You can offer such services on Fiverr and create unique designs for your clients. Having a few templates to show will help them choose a design or an idea for the design.

E-book Covers

The business of self-publishing is growing rapidly. So what better way to make money than by offering a gig in which you create their covers? Tap into your creativity and design an eye catching cover! There are many ways to include extras such as purchasing a premium image for them, designing the cover for a paperback version of the book and so much more. Just explore current Fiverr gigs for creating covers to get an idea of the kind of covers buyers are looking for!

Note that these are just some of the options available on Fiverr and are not limited to just these. You can look up some other options as well and exploit them.

Chapter 7: Mistakes to Avoid On Fiverr

When it comes to making it big on Fiverr, there are some mistakes that you have to avoid. In this chapter, we will look at some of these mistakes and how you can avoid them.

Poor gigs

It is important for you to set up an impressive gig on Fiverr if you wish to find good work. The gig should be such that it immediately catches your client's fancy. Your gig should be a true representation of your work and contain a selection of best works. Remember that your clients will form an opinion about your work based on what they see first. So, you should put up the best work for them to see. There is debate over what your best work really is. Some put up work that they think is impressive while others put up the ones that have garnered them rave reviews from the clients. That choice is yours to make but in general, the latter is a good choice, as your clients will prefer to see the work that others have liked in the past.

Old work

You should try to advertise your latest work in order for people to see. There are some people that prefer to hold on to old work as they think it is their best. But you have to try and update your work from time to time and put up the latest work. If you think your old work is good, then you can use only the best one and also add in samples of your other newest work.

Overdoing it

Sometimes, it is better to remain a little subtle instead of going all out and over doing your gig. Don't do too much as that will only distract your client. They won't know what to look at and decide to reconsider. Keep it simple yet informative. Don't add in too much description and try to get straight to the point. You have to edit your samples a little to make them look like figments of your actual work. Do not make the mistake of mentioning things you don't want the client to know about. It is always best to not mention things that you think will anyway go unnoticed, especially if it is just a small detail.

Pricing high

Some people turn over confident as soon as they land their first project and start over-pricing their services. That is the wrong way to go about it. You have to slowly and gradually increase your price. Even if you have now undervalued your services, you cannot rush to correct it. Wait for a month or two and then increase your pricing. You have to go slow and not be in a hurry to make thousands of dollars. You will know when to raise the stakes based on the reviews that you get and also how your competitors are pricing their services. You should be in it for the long term.

Hidden costs

One important thing to consider is *hidden costs*. Your clients will not like it if you charge them extra after the work is submitted. Many people on Fiverr have the practice of hiding a few costs, which they will only mention once the job is done. Your client might pay it without putting up a fight but might not return to you for service again. Remember that 1 old customer is as good as 10 new ones and so; you have to try to hold on to your old customers as much as possible. Remain as transparent about all the costs as possible and mention them explicitly.

Copying

Some people look at other people's work and end up emulating it. That will only cause you to produce clones of other people's work. In this day and age where everybody wants something unique, it would be a mistake to copy others. Your work should be unique and must stand out from the rest. You can go through some of what others have put up and then create your content. If you really like what someone else has done, then maybe you can use it as inspiration but not entirely copy from it.

Not spreading the word

No work will be good enough to do its own marketing. Even if you are a top class skills man, you have to spread the word about it in order for people to know. You have to put in effort to get word of your gigs out there and let people know what you are up to. You have to make use of your social media presence for the same and keep sharing videos and photos of your work. At the least, you can incorporate the links of your gigs on Fiverr. Tell as many people as possible in order to attract maximum customers.

Bad reviews

Bad reviews are the most dreaded aspects of Fiverr. Getting a bad review will definitely affect your confidence and also make you wonder about the repercussions. Therefore, you have to try and avoid getting a bad review as much as possible. If it is in your power, you should cancel the order if you think a bad review is on its way. We looked at this very aspect in detail earlier in the book and you should follow it keenly to help your Fiverr business take shape.

Going outside Fiverr

There will be some clients that will ask you if they can pay you outside Fiverr. That is a risky proposition, as you might not know whether the person will pay you after the job is done. It is best that you get the client to pay you through Fiverr itself. If something goes wrong and despite submitting the work the client does not pay you, then Fiverr will step in and help you out. Even if you think that the person is honest, you will be taking a big risk by agreeing to getting paid outside of Fiverr.

No diversity

Diversity is extremely important when it comes to showcasing your work and talent. Do not keep everything boring and typical. You have to surprise your clients in order to get them notice you. You should incorporate the latest trends as well so that you will be up to date with all your styles and trends.

High hopes

It is not a bad thing to dream big. You will feel quite confident if you have a good business. But expecting to see overnight results is not the way to go about it. You have to set goals for yourself and then go after them. If you have unreasonable expectations, then you are sure to pressurize yourself and be disappointed in the end. So, it is best to write down a few reasonable goals and start ticking them off as soon as they are attained. It will seem a little daunting at the very beginning no doubt but as and when your business starts to roll, you will start settling in with it and your goals will start getting ticked off.

These form the different Fiverr mistakes that you have to avoid in order to set up a stellar business.

Safety

It is important to remain safe and so, don't give away any personal information on the site. The client will not need your phone number or address as he or she can contact you directly on Fiverr. It is also important to not giveaway your bank account details to anyone, including your clients. They might end up misusing it. Your account details will be safe with Fiverr. You should also check the client's profile before taking up a job to ensure that they are genuinely interested in the deal and are not rivals looking to foil your efforts.

No fakes

Amazon issued a lawsuit against 1114 Fiverr sellers who provided fake reviews for products and services. So, it is important for you to steer clear of such controversies if you wish to remain good with your Fiverr business. Most of these sellers offer to write either good/ positive reviews for their clients on amazon or bad/ negative ones for the products or books that the client shares with the seller. If you have any such requests coming your way, then you should refuse to do it and can also show it to customer support. Use your moral judgment in determining whether or not the gigs and services you offer may breach any terms of services.

Write "anything"

It is important to be specific on Fiverr. Being too generic might cause the potential customer to walk away. If you say you can write "anything", it is important for you to specify the term. You have to tell them the different topics that you are comfortable with and can write easily on. There will be categories to choose from that will make it easier for you to pick the topics and also easy for the client to find you.

Limit it

Don't bite more than you can chew! It is best to take only so much work, which you can handle with ease. Taking too many will cause you to feel frustrated and might compromise on the quality of the work. Initially, it is better to go slow and see how many projects you can complete in a month. If you think you can do more, then you can go a bit faster and take a few more projects. If at any time you feel like there are too many on your hand, you can ask each one for a little extra time and try your best to finish them instead of cancelling. You will learn to be a bit more careful the next time.

Do your best!

It is extremely important for you to give your best regardless of whether you are getting paid $5 or $10. Don't think about the price. It is obvious that you will have to work for a small sum at the very beginning. It will not continue for long and you can always increase the price with time, as and when you start earning the badges. Also, you will have the chance to accrue a lot of experience and learn several things, which will help you better your skills.

Chapter 8: The Importance of Scaling and Automating Gigs

Now, when it comes to being on Fiverr, you've got to make sure that you're scaling on your gigs in an effective way. For some people, scaling gigs can be the difference between overdoing it and not overdoing it, between actually having time for everything you want to do and getting out the orders in a timely manner, and not doing it. You should also know a bit about automating gigs as well, as it can be an integral part of improving your income. All too often, those who start on Fiverr end up having the problem if they overwork themselves by not actually looking at the amount of gigs that you have and then scaling them accordingly.

What is Scaling

Scaling is a simple matter in a sense. Have you ever heard of people scaling back on gigs such as with shows and such in order to accommodate for any problems that might arise? It's a good way to measure how much work you can take, and having a scaling of just how many gigs you are taking each month can be the difference between being an overwhelmed entrepreneur and someone who is handling all of this.

Scaling is used to see how many gigs you can take in order to be the most efficient with your time and make the most money. Simply put, it's making sure you're not wasting your time and losing money in the process. Many times, people use this to help gauge your ability to really get things done.

It also is used to help up the prices in a fair manner if you're doing something that is way more than five dollars. For example, let's take someone who writes 500-word articles for 5 dollars each. Now, if you by chance take on ones that are 1000 words, but they are still being paid out as five dollars, that's not really very fair. Scaling is so important, because it can mean the difference between keeping your business going and losing a ton of money from this.

A lot of people who start out on Fiverr think it's smart to just let everything be five bucks, but the truth is, if the product is worth more than you're getting for it, you're entitled to fair pay. Obviously that's true with just about anything, which is why a price scale has to be there.

You have to let your clients know of the scale. Because if not, they won't know that they'll have to pay more, and you might end up doing a 2000-word article for five bucks instead of the twenty you feel like you deserve.

Let's take another example as well. Let's say you design book covers, and for five bucks you do the standard book cover that takes a little bit of time to do but is mainly just stock images that you find online and piece together. Not that involved. But let's say you know the market is looking for covers that are a bit more involved, a bit deeper than just your average little cover that's on one of those cheap romance books. You don't feel five dollars will do the product justice, and you want to ask for more. That's where the price scaling comes in. You can control just how much you're paying through this, and in turn, you'll get a fair amount of money that you feel you deserve as well.

Now, in a way of business thinking, the scaling has a variety of reasons for it. The scaling can be seen to also demonstrate the possibility of growth and the growth revenue with less costs in the operation of this. Basically it's increasing or decreasing your product value in order to accommodate and not lose out on the product costs.

Do businesses do this?

This is a simple question with a simple answer. Yes, all businesses do this in a sense. Let's think about it with an example. Let's say you work for a graphic design company that has you getting paid a certain amount for some work. Let's say that the operating costs increase, and so you increase the price of the work that you're doing.

Even with shopping centers and retail you get this. Inflation is the cost of increased costs in many stores, and it's why something that used to be a certain price a long time ago has now jumped in price. It's not because the company is trying to spite you, but rather it's because they need to accommodate for the losses.

Scaling in a business gives the company a chance to optimally use their resources and manage them across all of their fronts in order to reach a goal, whether that is income, production, or sales goals. It's the operation costs and revenue of a company, and it's the relationship between these things. Your ideal state should always be having the operational costs decrease while keeping the revenue increasing. Otherwise, you will go insolvent

How do you Use This?

You're probably looking at this and at this point probably thinking "great, how am I going to use this?" In essence, it's actually very easy to use, and you can apply this to pretty much any gig on Fiverr. You will learn how to effectively scale, and what you need to consider before you start to put in price increases and scaling.

- The first is value. Value is something that every product should have, and it's one of the biggest things you've got to remember and understand before you start to scale your business and change the prices. You need to see if whatever it is you are doing is actually something of value. Are you delivering a good and useful product to people? Or is it just something that's mediocre and not worth the money? Before you start to push the idea of business growth, you need to know if it has the repute needed to push it forward, along with the value that will turn over a profit for you in the long run. You should have a business model in place and take into consideration all of the actions you are doing and see if they fit into the business model.

- Marketplaces are another place to start looking at. Once you have the sales model in place, you should start to invest in and start to increase and scale the business. If you're building a team or increasing the business, you can definitely generate more profit. You're probably wondering if you should hire more people. We'll get into hiring later on, but in this case, you can use marketplaces to help with the costs of your company. You can dabble into more pools and get more from this. Let's take for example that you're a creative writer. You might have been writing romance for a while, and maybe dabbling in articles. It's time to showcase your talents in other fronts and start to increase the marketplaces. You'll want to do that. Make your prices competitive, but worth the costs, and you'll be able to increase your business without having to push further operational costs as well. You can have simple $5 gigs, but you should also keep in mind that you can increase these as well depending on the production you want to push forward, and how you can do this to really improve your sales over time.

- Inbound marketing is another great way to really help you get out and feel for things. You might not be able to do outbound marketing, so instead attract the customers without having to chase after them and wait on them with hand and foot. To do this, it's actually pretty simple. What you want to do is have an online presence established and then show off content that shows the different expertise. For many who use Fiverr to make money online, they will sue other social media channels in order to accomplish this. They might even have their own website as well, and even some loyalty programs to help with returning customers to come back. You can use your current people to help attract other people, and you won't come across desperate when looking for others, and plus, it saves you a boatload of time as well.

The Importance of Project Management

Now, it's not just you going out there and looking for new people to hire you for gigs, it's also your own personal project management as well. You might not have a lot of people working under you, but it's important to start to manage everything. In order to scale your business, you will have to make the most out of the resources you do have in order to improve the revenue. Let's say that you're a one-man operation. You might think you're operating at your best, but really take a look at yourself. See if you are, and if not, start to invest in project management tools. For example, there is one called Trello that allows you to manage your team if you have one. Start to use planners, calendars, and other planning tools of the like such as Asana to help you really get the most out of your business. When you hire others, do work to communicate with them and start to check up on them without having to do it yourself. Start to implement them and increase your productivity.

If you are working alone, you'll need to plan out and use your time effectively. If you don't use your time effectively, you will start to suffer from many problems. All too often, for those who are starting out on Fiverr, the problem isn't necessarily the gigs, but rather it's not having the time to do it all. Plan out your day, work on this, and at the end of it, you will have a better grip on everything and you'll be able to handle it all.

Automate for Success

Now, it's time we talk about another facet that can save your business. Automating. What this is, is you automatically deliver or do something with the product and have it whenever possible. Now, you might for example have courses online that you send to people if they pay five dollars. You can automate this by using some software and then sending it out to people. This in turn will increase the efficiency of the business.

You might be wondering why you would do this of all things. Well, let's take a look at a business in general. Let's say you have a business, and you're losing out on money. Maybe when you start to inspect where you're losing out, you notice you have one person sitting there and sending out the emails to people with the course. Let me tell you, that's not going to help you when you're sending this out to others. You might have a business that's doing amazingly, but if you have that labor cost there, you're going to end up losing a lot of money, and the cost might be what kills you. What you need to do is to nix that part of it, and start to instead push for automating everything where you can.

The best way to do this is to start looking into software to help you automate everything where you can. Now, for article and creative writing, you might not be able to do that due to the creative nature of things, but look for the ways to really improve your business. Take all of the mundane tasks that you will have at hand and get rid of them. If you have to send out confirmation emails, automate that. If you're sending out order numbers and times, automate that when you can. You can do this to help improve the speed of your business, and it dramatically increases efficiency.

Now, this isn't just sending out autoresponders or even email catches. This can also be something as simple as a customer support system, where they fill out the problem on a ticket and the best response is given to them. You can also add an FAQ page or even some help for the site or business. If you have people coming to you clamoring for the same question a billion times, it's not only annoying to answer each time, it will also make you made. Don't let that get you down, and instead automate it by giving the answers to most of the general questions there. Some people might not be able to read that and they might miss the point entirely, but when that happens, the simple answer is to just send them the FAQ once again and then go from there.

Finally, there is even social media and online portals you can use in order to help you with your scaling and automating. If you have a job, such as photo editing for people's pictures, and you have a whole variety of options that you could do for the pictures, instead of sending them out time and time again in a billion emails, you can instead create a google portal where people wills schedule the actions with you, and they will give you the photo and exactly what you need. This will save you a boatload of time, and it definitely will make it easier.

For social media reasons, you can save time by installing Hootsuite to help integrate all of your social media streams together, scheduling posts like how you can with Facebook and Tumblr, and you can even do that with Instagram as well. Social media updates don't have to be something you spend a ton of time focusing on, but instead start to automate it, and it will in turn save you time.

Automating for success is a great part of scaling. It saves you a ton of money, and you'll be able to help make more from this as well. Remember, scaling will help you increase your revenue without sacrificing production costs, so do that for yourself, work on that, and in turn, you'll be able to have a greater success as a result.

Chapter 9: Virtual Assistants and How They Can Help

A virtual assistant is a necessary part of some people's marketing strategies, and it will allow you to really improve the scaling of your business. What some don't know is that a virtual assistant is a godsend for some tasks, but you do need to find the right person. This chapter will go over the benefits of hiring a virtual assistant, what a virtual assistant is, and some of the tips to help you find the best person for the job.

What is a Virtual Assistant

A virtual assistant is someone that can help you with our business and help you keep the growth managed. Now, when a business starts to grow, we typically love to bite off more than we can chew. We start to see the orders pile up, with deadlines that stare at you right in the face like they're a monster, and customers are expecting it to be fast, because often when you start out, you have the ability to get the orders done super fast.

Now, this is where the problems arise. You might have been able to handle it all beforehand, but in truth, ever since you started getting more and more orders from people you haven't been able to handle it. You might instead hire some employees, but they're not the right people, and they don't seem to fit the bill. You might not be able to really have the abilities that you need to help streamline the business with these employees. Many of these employees are the types of people who aren't very good at handling the managing aspects of this, but there is one thing that you can use.

You can use a virtual assistant to help with the job. A virtual assistant is basically someone who controls most of the administrative functions of the job. Let's say that you're a book publishing company, you've got the writers, but you need some help with the nitty gritty. Well, these virtual assistants can sweep in so that you can have time to do what you need to grow the business.

This is also good for those who are on Fiverr and need some help with the administrative aspects of things. For many Fiverr businesses, the initial idea of success on Fiverr is to be getting money. You might be doing that, but then it becomes overwhelming. You don't have time to talk with customer support tags, or send out the courses for another flow of work, or any of that. You might have video series that people clamor for, and you don't have time to do that. Many times, hiring a normal employee comes with the stigma of they're only doing this to get a paycheck, and they don't want to worry about the quality of work. However, a virtual assistant can help you maintain the chaos while still allowing your business to grow in an extreme manner.

The virtual assistants help with many of the housekeeping aspects of a business. Things that you don't want to work on, or even chasing up employees and orders, can all be done by this person. They don't even have to be in the same space as you, but rather, they are the assistants that you need in order to help you keep your business going.

Now it might be hard for some at first. This person will work with you, and they might run you in a sense. But their goal is the same as yours, an improved business, and it's something that you will want to have as a result.

How to Hire One

Now, when it comes to hiring a virtual assistant, there are some things that you will need to keep in mind. For many people, they presume that hiring a virtual assistant is simple, and while it is, there are a few things that you have to keep in mind. You will discover the important parts of a virtual assistant and exactly what they should be doing in this section.

The first thing is their reliability. This is the most important part of it, and it's what you will need to watch out for. Are they reliable? Do they have good history? You can typically find freelance VAs on some of the hiring sites like Elance and Upwork, but you should also keep in mind that the person has to have a good track record of this. You should, when you're hiring someone, look at their credentials, see if they can do the work that you're needing, and really just make sure that you have it all squared away before you start to go on the hiring adventure. Reliability is something that you've first got to look for.

A successful work history is something else that you will want to look into. For many people, a successful work history is the difference between getting hired and getting the job done or not. All too often, people will hire these people that they thought were a good idea. But in truth, they have no experience, so in essence, they're only hurting themselves. The same goes for people who hire these virtual assistants that have no experience. It will be like training an employee all over again, which is something that you shouldn't have to do. This person isn't your average employee, so don't treat him like that, and instead get someone who is reliable and useful.

You should also look at the rate of the assistants. You'll have to pay them, but you can control how much they are paid based on how much they desire. You should determine what your budget is from the onset, and then look for people who have the experience and success needed for this. If your budget is low, you might end up getting people who don't fit the budget, but you can adjust this accordingly if you are starting to have issues with it as well.

You should also find a virtual assistant that fits you. If you need someone around all the time, hire someone who is willing to answer messages late at night. If you're a morning person, have a VA that is on the same time zone you are, or relatively close, and then work from there. You can give them tasks, and they will do them for you, but you should find one that works for you.

Do interview them, but you won't have to spend a ton of time like you would with a normal employee. Look at them, check their track record, and make sure that they can do all the tasks listed. It's never a fun situation when you hire on a VA and they end up having more trouble attracted to them than they are worth. You don't need the gray hairs that come with bad VAs, just like how you don't need that with bad employees. Remember, they are here to help your business, and they work hard to help scale the business and take it to new heights.

The Benefits of Virtual Assistants

Now, virtual assistants have their own set of benefits that will help you. You should know this if you're still not convinced about getting one, but you should be relatively sold on the element of a VA at this point. This section will go over the benefits of hiring a virtual assistant

High quality is your first and foremost benefit. Now, a VA is typically more productive and will give you more value than the other employees you might have had in the past. These assistants are committed to what they need to do, and they want to please you. They want to meet and exceed the expectations. Now, you might have these people on a long-term contract, or on short-term contracts. Whatever it may be, you'll set the time you'll need them, and they will work hard so that you do give them a chance to work for you again. This is in contrast to the typical employee who knows they have a secured job and they do the secured job to a mediocre expectation. There is also the benefit that these Virtual assistants are typically trained in whatever niche you need them in to help with the productivity. In short, every single virtual assistant that you have is an expert in a sense, and their experience will help to bring you to a higher level and in turn will give you a greater business. It's pretty awesome, and that alone is a major benefit that they have.

Then there is the sheer convenience of them. Virtual assistants are the types of people who work differing schedules, so it's not like they only work during the day and then you're screwed at night. A virtual assistant can be used for an evening, or you need some help for a season, or even for just the weekend. A virtual assistant is a great tool because they can work with the staff during busy times or when they need help with the other tasks. If you have a ton of orders that you have to complete, a virtual assistant can be hired on to help offset the workload while still helping you get it out the door in a timely manner. Plus, you can have one on call for when you need to execute tasks fast.

The cost of them is definitely a great thing that can help with your business. They are cost-effective on many levels. You don't have to spend money on benefits, taxes, give office space, or even train them. They just give the money to them when they finish the project, and you don't have to put too much effort forward for them. For those who are on Fiverr and don't have the money to pay for benefits and such, this is something that you can use that will not be super pricy, but you'll also get the work out the door to great results.

Then there are the skills of a VA. A VA actually has a diverse skill set. In truth, they train themselves to do the jobs that they will need. Sometimes, people think that having a monoculture is good, but in truth it will just stagger your business. Having a VA who has experience and who has worked on many projects in tons of different industries can give you added insight and give you thoughts to the table for future projects. For many who work with them, it gives new ideas and even a fresh and interesting perspective that they can provide. They might show you things that even you weren't sure of.

Then there is business growth. This is something that is typically underrated in terms of what a VA can do for you. For many people, this gets overlooked, but these Virtual assistants that you hire will take care of the daily tasks that you need done, and you'll be able to focus on what matters. The tedium of the business will be taken out of your repertoire, and you'll be scaling with these people in your arsenal as well. You in turn will grow your business exponentially, and you'll be taking home more money. At the end of the day, everyone wins, and in truth, it's definitely a benefit that can help save you money.

This goes along with scaling, but it is also something that you should have for when the orders become too much for just you alone. A virtual assistant can be the best choice that you've ever made in a business, and you'll be able to definitely get a whole lot of benefits out of this, and it can take your business to the level that it deserves quickly, and without causing you to lose a ton of money.

Chapter 10: Advanced Fiverr Marketing Tips for Success

Now that you know a lot about Fiverr and just what it can do for you, there is the aspect of marketing that you will need to keep in mind. Marketing is something that will be a major factor in the survival of your business, for you have to market to others in order to really be successful. With Fiverr, you will need to market in order to get new customers, and while you might think it's easy at first, in truth, it does take a bit of work to really be successful with it. There are basic marketing tips you can utilize, but this chapter will go over on the advanced tips that will assist you in making the most out of your Fiverr experience so you'll be able to make more money.

1) A Picture speaks a thousand words: this is one of the most important, but often left out tips that people can use. If you're trying to sell a gig on Fiverr, include pictures of your gigs to show off to others what you've done in your previous gigs. If you have a profile picture, make sure it's a real photo. Many people are still wary of the Internet, and they need to be reassured that the person that is working with them is real. Don't just have any avatar, especially not a cartoon or other sort of thing unless you're showing off your graphic design. You should keep the profile picture something that is professional, so that you're seen as a professional to others

2) Keep it fast: now the element of speed is what will get you money. People on Fiverr like things done fast, and they will go for people that finish gigs fast. They will search for those that have reputations of being fast, and many times they will look for those that can have it within the day. Now, what you should do is to talk with the client and have the questions ready, making sure that you have everything that you need and

also get whatever sorts of various actions they need for the gig right away. Work fast, within a day if you can, and always submit it 24 hours before your deadline. Production speed is a great marketing tool, and it will show others that you are fast, and that you deliver great work.

3) Keep gigs active: if you're trying to keep gigs active, make sure that they are a list of gigs that show off your skills. You should have at least five to ten of them active, and definitely offer a wide variety of the gigs that you can do. This can help you demonstrate the various skills you have and what you will provide. It also might show you new channels on where to market, and with that, you'll be able to really get the marketing you need out there. Don't be afraid to show off your skills and definitely make sure they are of a high quality.

4) Professionalism is key: now with this, a great marketing tool in it of itself is having a professional service actually be professional. Deliver it to the highest quality that you can, do it fast, and be respectful with customers. Many times, people will look at the quality of the seller alone before you even get a chance to work with them, and it might be a difference between having the gig and not having the gig. So be professional, give quality, and do make it the best gig that you can so that sellers will come back for more.

5) Ask for feedback: feedback is so important on Fiverr. It's important on pretty much any selling channel, because it can show others that the person that they're hiring does a good job, and what they need to look out for. On Amazon for example, product feedback allows the person to know what they're getting before they buy the product, and sometimes, the lack of product will be what turns people away from buying the product in general. Don't let it stop you, and instead ask after the gig is over to provide feedback and even ask them in an email to do so.

6) Create an email list: if you have returning customers, ask them if they want to be a part of an email list. Put them in there, and then, once a month send out emails about your services. You can even inform them of new services that are being rendered, and you can make it so that they're the first to know. You can do preorder sales as well, similar to what people will do with games and such, where they will order the service, and then they're the first to get it. Think of it as a customer perk, and it will in turn bring in more recurring customers, and they can also bring in others.

7) Referral program: a referral program can be used with nearly any sort of marketing outlet, but with Fiverr, it does something magical. With Fiverr, the more people you have for a gig, the more it'll show. Let's say you do a gig for a person, they love it, and then after you ask for them to refer a person. They refer a person to you, and then they work with you. You can offer a perk, such as maybe a free article or service with a referral that orders something, and in turn, this will grow your outlets so that you have more to market to. Being able to refer others can really help you use this service in order to make money, and it's a technique that's used on many sites, but with Fiverr it does wonders.

8) Join Twitter: Twitter is a great place to market, but it works especially well for those on Fiverr. The reason for this is because twitter isn't just used for a business, but it can also be used for PR that you might not be able to get otherwise. For example, major changes in your gigs and other such factors can be showcased on Fiverr, and even success stories can be shown to people. If you're on twitter, you will get attention in as simple as talking with other people that are like-minded and building tweets. You'll be able to get the notice you want, and you can work with others.

9) Be eye-catching: Branding is very important, because it can show others who you are and what you're like. But what you need as well is a decorative logo or something to help others remember you. Now, for your profile you should keep your picture as a picture of yourself, but show off your logo so that others remember you. Maybe even write a slogan or something underneath it to help others see you again. It's a hard task, but if you have the right logo it will pull in other people like flies to honey. It will capture the attention that you want, and in turn, it will be even better success.

10) Don't Waste Resources: A common problem that many people do when they get started is they try to push the outreach more than anything. You should instead try to put out attention-grabbing strategies. You should instead start on getting attention through social media marketing and production, and from there, you'll be able to continue. You shouldn't get a PR firm involved in your business, but instead do the PR yourself when necessary, and instead try to promote yourself in the most eye-catching of ways.

11) Adding graphics to social media: this goes in a similar vein as to the importance of pictures before, but instead push it into online marketing. If what you're doing immediately is just writing text, you should improve your marketing through the use of pictures. Show off your product; maybe even have a slogan or joke attached to it. Be creative with this, for the graphics can help you really reach out to other people, and it can make online marketing even better. A picture is worth a thousand words, and sometimes using that in social media can mean the difference between a customer not being attracted and one being attracted.

12) Create ad campaigns: now, Facebook ads are pretty hit or miss, but if you want to, you can start to push forward your ads and various media on other social media outlets, such as

Twitter and Instagram. Both are strong contenders with getting the customer attention. Sometimes, Facebook ads can help with getting the clicks to your gigs. For many brands, they've found that Facebook advertising does work in some cases, but it does help mostly with customers who are looking for your brand through this advertising. You can use social media sites to help get the momentum that you need in order to help you market to success.

13) Get the right attention: you want to get the right attention from the right people. Choose the audience that you want for this, and start to market to them. If you keep the attention in the right place, and to people who are interested, they will want to work with you as well.

14) Cooperate with media: now, let's say that you have the right connections because of a previous gig or in general. You can use media, or other businesses, and you can work together to help gain the attention that you want. It can be hard to work with these, so do ask them nicely with a small email on some of the benefits that your product has for others, and you can maybe collaborate together to help get the success that you want.

15) Collaborate with other sellers: it doesn't always have to be a competition, but if you get the right kind of collaboration, you can be successful. Collaborating with other artists, in the case of those who sell art gigs on Fiverr, or even just working together, can help you increase your fan base and improve the marketing. You should find someone who is not a direct competitor, and who would be willing to work together with you. Maybe you two can trade services and even help improve the other's attention with their audience. Sometimes collaborating and working together can be the best marketing tool that you have, because although it might be seen as a competition, it doesn't always have to be, that's for sure.

16) Reach out to cold customers: now, this might be something that you might not be ready for right away, but over time, reaching out to new people and introducing your service with social media can be helpful. Let's say that you see someone who is interested and likes your content a lot. On Twitter, you can direct message them, and maybe you can ask them if they want more information. If you see someone who is slightly interested, then start to go for it. Remember, marketing isn't always the easy part, and sometimes you have to swallow your fear of talking with other people and just go for it to help make a new customer for your gigs.

17) Reward customers with cash towards a next purchase: sometimes, giving them a small discount will make them come back. This is almost a surefire way to get customers to come back to you. You can send them cash that can be redeemed with the next purchase, such as maybe a dollar or something, or you can also do it in the form of coupons. You should also put in any of the specifics such as the expiration date and the details. Give it to the customers in an email, and they can put it in the next time they work with you. Coupon codes are also important with this as well, so don't forget to implement it.

18) Offer holiday incentives: when the holidays roll around, it seems that everyone is interested in trying to get new customers. You can use various holidays, not just Christmas for example, to help gain customers and get more sales. You can offer coupons from time to time for holidays, and if you offer a service that coincides well with one certain holiday, put it in there. Don't be afraid to offer coupons for the right times, because it can help customers come back to you again and again for more.

19) Talk to customers: don't be afraid to talk with your customers. It can be as simple as getting the specifics on the job, or you can even talk with them through email and social media. It's a

good way to get to know the consumers that you have in front of you. This also helps with other such insights as well, such as what sells, what they liked, and what you can do in order to help improve their experience. You want to get to know these people, so it might be a bit scary to do so initially, but it can be something that will help you.

20) Start a blog: a blog is something that can help you immensely with social media presence, and getting customers to go to your Fiverr site, along with even expanding into future areas. The leads that you generate here can go to many different fronts, and it can help with Fiverr sales. If you are going to start a blog, start with an idea of where you want to go with this. Maybe you're selling various graphic design services, and you use the blog to not only promote your service, but also go over latest news and opinion pieces on various graphic design ideas. You should use your blog to help generate a fan base, and in turn, you can then use the people that you're catching to lead them to your Fiverr site, and from there, you can get further orders from people as well.

21) Use SEO: now SEO does play a part in this. Search engine optimization is used for just about anyone who is a business owner in this day and age. You want to know where you rank in terms of the competition and where in google searches you are. You should know where you're landing, because that might not be where you're getting or not getting customers. Writing pieces with the right keywords, using the correct keywords in your gigs, all of this is something that will make a difference between whether or not you're getting customers or not. You want to improve your SEO as much as possible. You can tweak a few things online, such as keywords and what you use, and from there, you can go from there. If you do struggle with this, you can use your virtual assistant or hire someone

who knows about SEO to assist you in your efforts, whatever you feel is right.

22) Content marketing: content parking is another aspect of marketing that you can use on Fiverr in order to help generate an audience and to market to others. Content marketing does connect the consumer to what your brand and what you are all about. This gives you a chance as well to allow you to speak with others as well, and content marketing has the ability to attract new customers as well, and you'll be reaching out to more customers than you expected. The content that you have will show off to the right people, and you'll be able to have content that is shared through social media in order to help you become more successful.

23) Survey your customers: sometimes a survey is a great marketing tool that will allow you to improve how other brands compare and how customers see you. You can find out what people are interested in, so that from there you're able to create the content that you need to create in order to help get the interest that you want to have. All too often, we go through businesses not really surveying to see what others like, what interests them, and other such things. If we're not careful, we might be marketing the wrong things to people. Instead of doing that, change it up, and start to include a survey at the end of your gigs so that people can fill it out and you can see what you need to improve in order to make it better:

24) Find the right audience: this is another step that you will need to take. When forming your brand, make sure that you're marketing to the right people. If you are using Instagram and your audience is a bunch of young women, don't start to market your content to older women, because it won't generate sales. Look at what you're offering, and then make a list of the types of audiences you should have when you're

marketing this. Who is going to buy the product? If you're not sure, look at the people who have already bought your product and from their start to make a list of the similarities of each of these people. From there you will be able to find the similar aspects of each, and then, you'll be able to market it successfully and without too many problems attached to it as well.

25) Build a community: if you build a community, you'll be able to build you brand. If you have a community and manage it, you'll definitely have people who are willing to talk to you and work with you. It's not easy, that's for sure, but it can be helpful in those who are looking for a frugal way to help save money and get the people that they want. You can build the community, and it can be a success.

These marketing strategies can help you build the business that you want, and it can make your dream of working on Fiverr without having to work another job a reality. Take these into consideration, use them, and in turn, you'll have way more success.

Chapter 11: How to Be Successful in a Gig Realm

Gigs are a bit hard to really push forward, and there are a few things that you can do in order to generate success with gigs. This chapter will go over a few aspects to keep in mind before you start on your journey to using Fiverr to sell services for success

The first is to see the world as an entrepreneur. You can go out and really see the world out there. When you build your business, you'll start to realize you don't have to work a typical job, so you can get out and see what the world has to offer. You can really do what you love anywhere you want as long as you use the right plan for your business. If you're serious about using Fiverr, you'll get to the point where you don't need to babysit it, and you can see what's out there while still making money.

Then there is the right type of selling. You can sell your creativity through Fiverr to help with your business efforts, and you can in turn streamline the process of it as well. Sometimes, when you're at the right point, you can invest in an eCommerce platform that will help you transition the sales and get them fast. If you do that, you'll be able to sell even more, and Fiverr gives you the chance to do that.

You should also look at both the creativity and the marketing. Sure, it's fun to write what you love, but if you're not careful, you might lose it all because of the marketing aspects of this. You've got to look at your business to see if it is growing well, and then nurture it, because if you let the business take a backseat in your life, it won't grow as well. You should grow the business to the level you want it to be, and avoid any pitfalls that can come up.

Now, you should look as well at the loyal customers. For those who are working on Fiverr and doing mainly that, new customers are always nice, but a repeat business can help a company way more so. Loyal customers are not just a good sort of income, but they are also the type of people you can recommend to other services, such as maybe you're leading your gigs from Fiverr to something more. Plus, these people will be able to sell you to others and help you with potential new customers. Just because a customer is a happy done doesn't mean they'll come back and buy from you again, but rather you need a strategy for this. You will want to cultivate it so that you can get more customers, and don't be afraid to get in there and really see if you can get to others as well.

Being smart about the way you market to other people can make a difference between a successful Fiverr business and an unsuccessful one. Don't limit your potential, and instead start to change the way you're looking at your mind, and from there, start to improve your life to the way it is supposed to be. You will have a much better experience once you get started on the path to success with Fiverr, and from there, you can make more money than you've ever expected to before.

Key Highlights

Fiverr is a great place to start earning a passive income. It is an online site that allows people to advertise their skills and get paid for providing service.

Fiverr is a free website where anyone can register and start using. It will not take you any more than 10 minutes to set up your account and can start creating gigs. Gigs refer to your sales pitch. They are samples that you create for your clients to see and also include a description of what you have on offer for them. These gigs are generally charged at $5, which is what gives the website its unique name.

There are many buyers and sellers on Fiverr and you will find it rather easy to find your clients. But before that, you have to advertise your gigs and tell people about your Fiverr venture. You can make use of social media to spread word and try incorporating links to your Fiverr pages as much as possible. It is important to try and make your presence felt on all social media platforms and also blog about it. You have to understand and make use of SEO.

There are certain pricing principles that you must understand which will help you price your work appropriately. There are badges that are given away to Fiverr sellers and each subsequent badge will allow you to raise the value at which you offer your service. If you get the pricing right, you stand a chance to make around $4,000+ a month.

We looked at some of the best gigs that you can set up. These will help you earn quite well, provided you are good at what you do. Also remember to ask your clients to give you a good rating as that will help you show up in the top 5 or 10 recommendations.

Ratings and reviews count quite a bit on Fiverr. You have to have good ratings and reviews in order to attract other customers. They will look at what ratings you have attained from your previous clients and also the reviews, which will act as testimonials. You also have the option of force cancelling an order if you think the client will leave behind a bad review.

It is obvious that you will not always have good reviews. If you have bad ones coming your way, you should check if the client is another seller on Fiverr trying to sabotage you. If so, then you can take the case up with Fiverr customer support, which will help you out. If the client is genuinely dissatisfied with your service then you should ask them to change their mind and give you at least an average review, as that will surely help your business.

We looked at some of the mistakes that you have to avoid on Fiverr if you wish to set up a successful business. You can go through it again of you like and avoid them at all costs. We also saw important notes that will help you conduct your business smoothly.

Remember to remain patient with your Fiverr endeavor and you will surely experience success!

Conclusion

I thank you once again for choosing this book and hope you had a good time reading it.

There are many ways in which you can use make money online but it is important to know the right way to go about it.

As you know, it is very easy for you to get started with Fiverr. You will not have to go through many procedures and can start fairly simply.

You have to remain a bit patient especially in the beginning, work hard and finally, you will have the chance to set up a successful online business.

There is no limit on the number of businesses that you can open up on Fiverr and earn a lot of money from each one!

Special Invitation!

If you liked what you read and would like to read high quality books, get free bonuses, and get notified first of **FREE EBOOKS,** then join the official Xcension Publishing Company Book Club! Membership is free, but space is limited!

You can join the Book Club by clicking the link below:

>>JOIN THE CLUB!!<<

FREE Bonus Videos!

As promised, here are your FREE Bonus Videos that will help you on your making your dream a reality by making money online! Good luck!

Just visit the link below to download the zip file containing the videos! If you are unable to download them, please e-mail promotion@xcensionpublishing.com to get the videos sent directly to you!

http://www.xcensionpublishing.com/FiverrVideos.zip

Printed in Great Britain
by Amazon